# TOYS
## THROUGH TIME

C H R I S   O X L A D E

MACDONALD YOUNG BOOKS

First published in 1995 by Macdonald Young Books Ltd

© Macdonald Young Books Ltd

Macdonald Young Books Ltd
Campus 400
Maylands Avenue
Hemel Hempstead
Herts HP2 7EZ

**Design and typesetting**: Roger Kohn Designs
**Illustration**: Coral Mula, Ross Watton
**Commissioning editor**: Debbie Fox
**Editor**: Caroline Wilson
**Picture Research**: Val Mulcahy
**Consultant**: Paul Atterbury

**Photo Acknowledgements**
We are grateful to the following for permission to
reproduce photographs: Antikenmuseum/Staatliche Museen
Preubischer Kulturbestiz, Berlin (photo: Johannes Laurentius),
p.8; The Bodleian Library, Oxford MS. Douce 8, p.6, p.12;
Clive Corless, p.14, p.22; Paul Mulcahy, p.36; The National
Trust Photographic Library, p.18; Robert Opie, p.28;
Sotheby's, p.32; VTECH Electronics (UK) plc, p.40

Sindy is a trademark owned by Hasbro U.K. and is used with
permission.

The publishers would like to thank the following for their
help: Clive Corless; LEGO U.K. Limited; Mark Mulcahy;
Helen Nolan; Sony Computer Entertainment Europe.

Printed and bound in Portugal by Ediçoes ASA.

ISBN 0 7500 1334 6

# CONTENTS

# THE FIRST TOYS

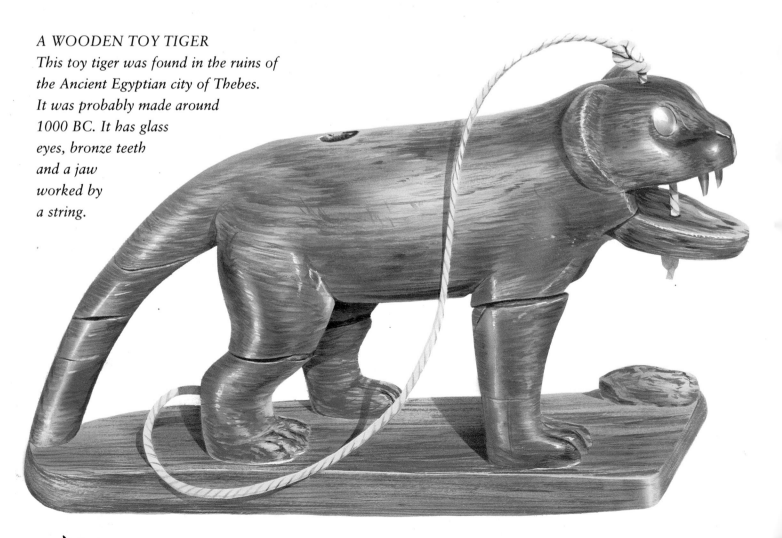

*Many ancient types of toy are still popular today. This vase from Ancient Greece shows a boy playing with a yo-yo.*

The earliest toys we know of were made over two thousand years ago in Ancient Egypt. Archaeologists have found toys such as balls, tops and dolls, in Egyptian tombs. The toys were intended for the dead person to play with in the next world, where the Egyptians believed their souls went when they died. Pictures of children playing with wheeled toys also appear on Egyptian wall paintings. The toys were all home-made from simple materials like clay, wood, and reeds from the banks of the River Nile. Children in Ancient Greece and Rome played with a wider range of toys than Egyptian children, including hobby horses and toy soldiers. Some were more complex in construction than Egyptian toys, but were still made from everyday materials.

*A WOODEN TOY TIGER*
*This toy tiger was found in the ruins of the Ancient Egyptian city of Thebes. It was probably made around 1000 BC. It has glass eyes, bronze teeth and a jaw worked by a string.*

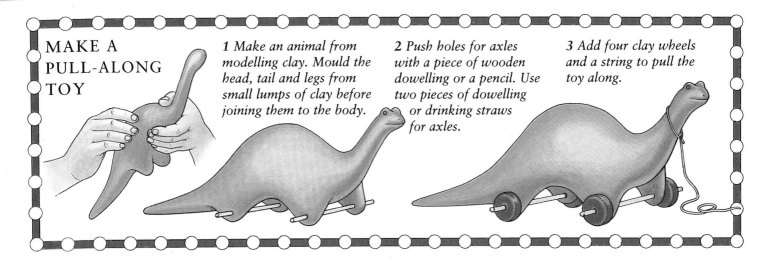

## MAKE A PULL-ALONG TOY

**1** Make an animal from modelling clay. Mould the head, tail and legs from small lumps of clay before joining them to the body.

**2** Push holes for axles with a piece of wooden dowelling or a pencil. Use two pieces of dowelling or drinking straws for axles.

**3** Add four clay wheels and a string to pull the toy along.

## CLAY FIGURES

Models of animals, people and different objects were popular ancient toys, just as they are today. The most versatile material for making these was clay. Adding wheels to a clay animal turned a model into a pull-along or push-along toy.

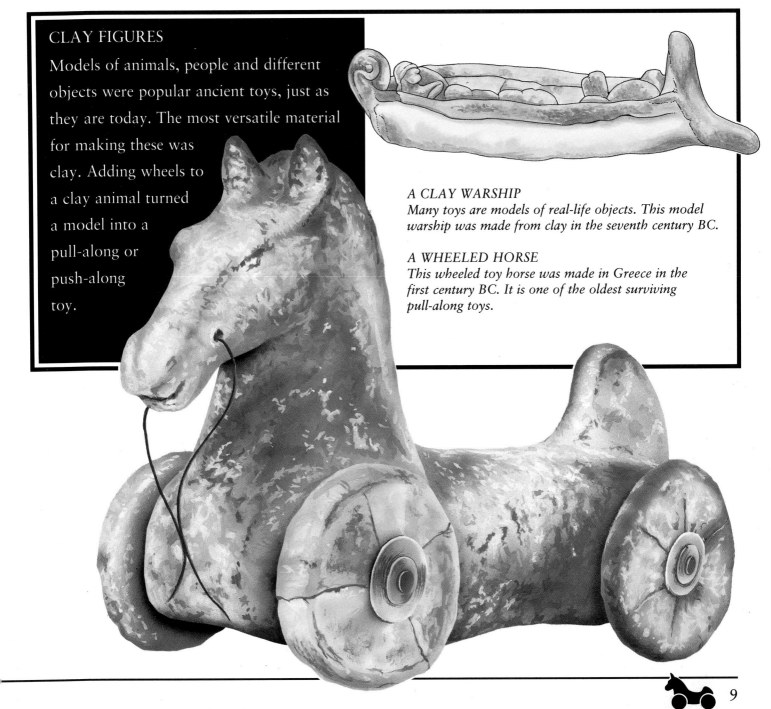

### A CLAY WARSHIP
Many toys are models of real-life objects. This model warship was made from clay in the seventh century BC.

### A WHEELED HORSE
This wheeled toy horse was made in Greece in the first century BC. It is one of the oldest surviving pull-along toys.

## SPINNING TOPS

The top is one of the oldest traditional toys. Once a top is spinning, its own weight stops it from falling over. Over the centuries, children have found several different ways of making tops spin.

## WAYS OF SPINNING A TOP

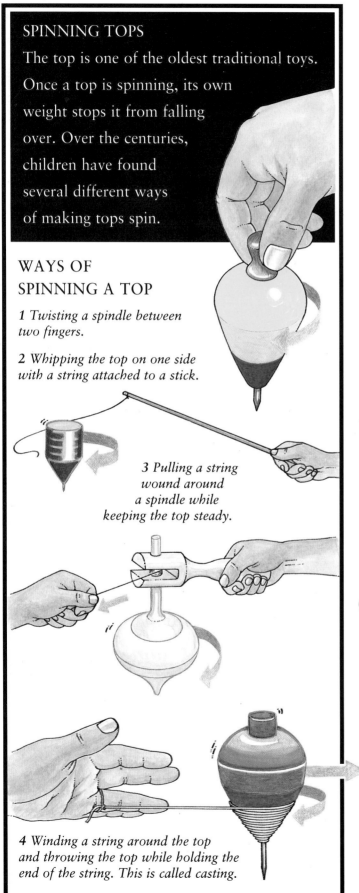

1 *Twisting a spindle between two fingers.*

2 *Whipping the top on one side with a string attached to a stick.*

3 *Pulling a string wound around a spindle while keeping the top steady.*

4 *Winding a string around the top and throwing the top while holding the end of the string. This is called casting.*

## SIMPLE TOYS OF TODAY

*A toy train made from corks, pins and wire.*

Children still make their own simple toys just as they did before there were toys to buy. They use simple materials, such as clay or wood, or even pieces of rubbish. The toys that children in one country make are often similar to those made by children in other countries. They are traditional toys, such as rag dolls or spinning tops, or models of everyday objects like telephones or cars. Toys like this can be highly decorated, with paints and coloured paper or fabric and yarn, or they can be left quite plain.

*This modern whip top from Bulgaria looks as if it could have been played with in the Middle Ages, and in fact the design has not changed for hundreds of years.*

## THE DEVELOPMENT OF TOPS

Simple tops have changed very little for hundreds of years, but there have been some innovations.

*AROUND 2000 BC
A clay spinning top from Ancient Egypt.*

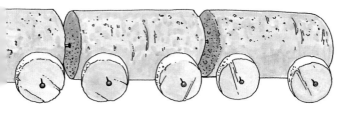

Small, simple toys, such as plastic figures, are often as much fun to play with as larger, more complicated toys. Small plastic toy parts can be made quickly and automatically by machines. This mass production means they are cheap to make and therefore cheap to buy. When you play with simple toys, you have to use your own imagination, just as children did thousands of years ago. As well as making them move, you can make up stories and adventures for them.

*Plastic doll models of characters from films and television programmes are very popular toys today. They normally have a few moving or interchangeable parts.*

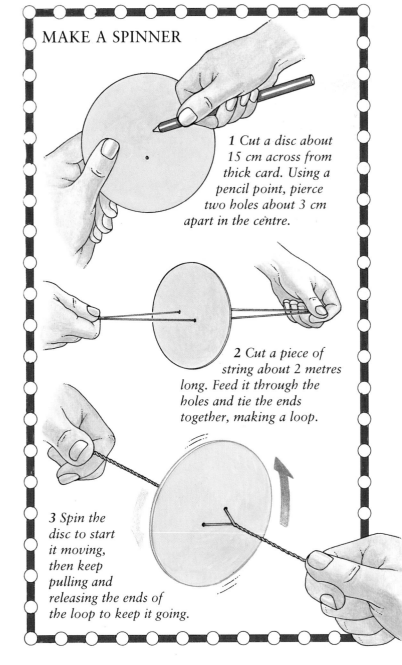

### MAKE A SPINNER

*1 Cut a disc about 15 cm across from thick card. Using a pencil point, pierce two holes about 3 cm apart in the centre.*

*2 Cut a piece of string about 2 metres long. Feed it through the holes and tie the ends together, making a loop.*

*3 Spin the disc to start it moving, then keep pulling and releasing the ends of the loop to keep it going.*

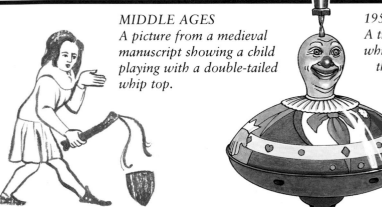

**MIDDLE AGES**
*A picture from a medieval manuscript showing a child playing with a double-tailed whip top.*

*1950s*
*A tin-plate plunger top, which is spun by pushing the spiral plunger up and down.*

*1970s*
*A gyroscope with a frame that stays still as the inner flywheel turns. The same principle is used in compasses for navigation.*

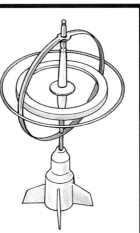

*TOY WINDMILLS*
*This picture is part of a sixteenth-century manuscript. The child is playing with a toy windmill.*

The Roman Empire came to an end in the fifth century AD. Historians call the next five hundred years the Dark Ages because Europe was plunged into chaos. There were frequent wars, and some skills and types of craftsmanship were lost or forgotten. Children had to make do with a few simple toys, such as rag dolls. After the Dark Ages, toy-making skills began to reappear. Craftsmen

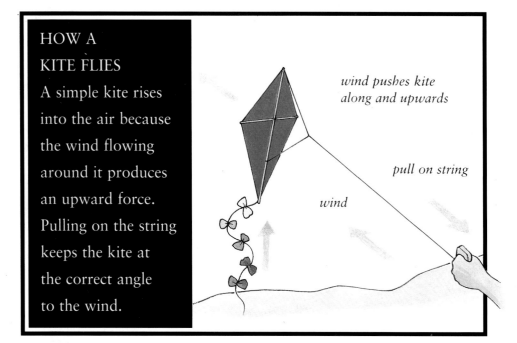

## HOW A KITE FLIES

A simple kite rises into the air because the wind flowing around it produces an upward force. Pulling on the string keeps the kite at the correct angle to the wind.

*wind pushes kite along and upwards*

*pull on string*

*wind*

*A JAPANESE FIGURE KITE*
*A traditional Japanese figure kite from the nineteenth century. Kites were popular toys in Japan and China because paper and bamboo were cheap materials.*

once again made toys to sell at markets and fairs. As well as the toys of the Romans, children also had new types of toys, including some that were powered by the wind, such as toy windmills and kites. In fact, kites were invented in China, probably as early as 200 BC. Kite-making ideas reached Europe in the late fourteenth century.

MAKE A PAPER WINDMILL

1 Cut a four-petalled flower shape from thick paper or thin card. Make it about 30 cm from top to bottom.

2 Cut down each petal to halfway, and fold one half to the middle. Push a drawing pin through the centre to keep the petals in place.

3 Push the drawing pin through a small bead into a wooden stick, and blow.

bead

pin

# TOYS FOR EVERYONE

*FLAT MODEL SOLDIERS*
*Three 'flat' model soldiers - a standard-bearer and two foot soldiers. They are about 5 cm high and 3 mm thick.*

From the fourteenth century onwards, European merchants began to trade more and more widely. Craftsmen began to manufacture things, including toys, in large numbers for export abroad. But most manufactured toys were still too expensive for ordinary people. Dolls' houses and other luxuries were only available to rich children.

By the eighteenth century, manufacturers were beginning to make toys from a variety of materials. Most were still made from wood, but soldiers and other figures were being cast in metals such as tin, lead and pewter. Other new toy-making materials were paper, papier mâché, china and tin-plate. Tin-plate is a thin sheet of steel covered in a very thin coat of tin. As manufacturing methods improved, toys began to get cheaper to buy.

*A PEWTER MONKEY*
*Pewter is an alloy (mixture) of tin and small amounts of other metals. Pewter was a common material because it was used for plates and cups until china and porcelain replaced it in the eighteenth century.*

*A 'LEAD FLAT' KNIGHT*
*The first metal toy soldiers were called 'flats' because they were flat models with detail on one or both sides.*

## HOW A 'FLAT' WAS MADE

**1** The contours of the model were carved in reverse into two slate blocks. The blocks were placed tightly together to make a hollow mould.

**2** Molten tin was poured through a small hole in the top of the mould.

**3** When the tin had cooled and turned solid, the mould was opened. The model was then welded to a tin base.

## HOW A TIN-PLATE MODEL WAS MADE

**1** The coloured decoration for both sides of the model was printed on to a flat sheet of tin-plate.

**2** The pieces were cut out and pressed into shape by machine.

**3** The pieces were joined together. This was done by bending small tabs on one piece around the edges of the next piece.

*PRESSED TIN-PLATE HORSE AND CARRIAGE*
*The earliest pressed tin-plate toys were cut from plain metal, but soon the tin-plate sheets were being printed with details before the pieces were pressed out. Tin-plate toys are still being made.*

## DESIGN A PAPER CUT-OUT MODEL

*1 First make a prototype model from scraps of paper and card. Use simple shapes joined together with tabs and slots.*

*2 Take your finished model apart. Press the pieces flat and arrange them on a piece of plain paper.*

*3 Trace round the shapes. Colour them in and add details like the eyes. Write instructions for making the model. Now see if a friend can make it without your help!*

## PAPER TOYS

In the eighteenth and nineteenth centuries, paper was widely used in toy-making. The most common paper toys were cut-out sheets. Printed shapes were sold in sheets. Children could stick these on to stiff card, cut them out, and join them together to make a finished toy. Theatres complete with scenery and actors, ships, and dolls supplied with a change of paper clothes were all popular types of cut-out sheet toys. Papier mâché was also used for making figures, and especially for moulding dolls' heads.

*A PAPER DOLL Paper dolls often came with dresses, wigs and hats - all in the latest fashions.*

## MATERIALS THROUGH THE AGES

Many different materials have been used for making toys. Here are a few of the most important ones.

*ANCIENT EGYPTIAN TIMES TO TODAY Clay, along with wood, was one of the first toy-making materials. Modelling clay is still popular.*

*SEVENTEENTH TO NINETEENTH CENTURIES A wax coating gave a doll's head and arms a life-like appearance.*

*A MODERN
SOFT TOY
Good-quality
soft toys have a
label showing
that they have
been made to a
strict standard.*

## DANGER AND SAFETY

Until the second half of the twentieth century, toys were made without much thought for children's safety. By today's standards, many of them would seem quite dangerous. In many countries there are now strict safety rules that toy manufacturers must follow by law. Soft toys, such as teddy bears, must not be made or stuffed with flammable materials, which could burst into flames if the toy were too near a fire. Toys for very young children must not have tiny pieces that a child could pull off and possibly swallow. Substances that we know are poisonous, like lead, are no longer allowed to be used in toy-making.

*1950s TO
TODAY
Plastic is
now the
main toy-
making
material.
There is more
about plastic
on pages 36-38.*

*1840s TO 1930s
Rubber was moulded
into dolls' heads,
animals and squeaking
toys. Then early plastics
like celluloid were used.*

## TEDDY BEARS

Toy bears had been popular for a hundred years before teddy bears appeared. They were much more realistic and stood on all fours. The first teddy bear was made in the United States in 1903. The design was based on a bear from a cartoon about President Roosevelt, whose nickname was Teddy. Bears subsequently became more furry and some were made with extra features like squeaks and growls.

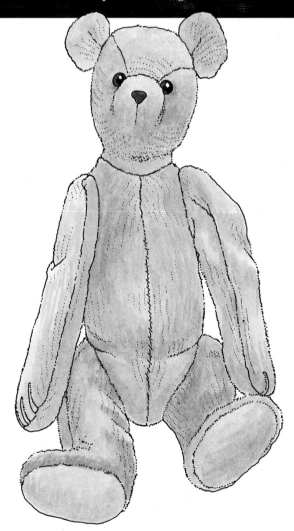

*This is one of the oldest teddy bears still in existence.
It was made in 1907, from hessian and cotton, and
was stuffed with sawdust.*

# DOLLS

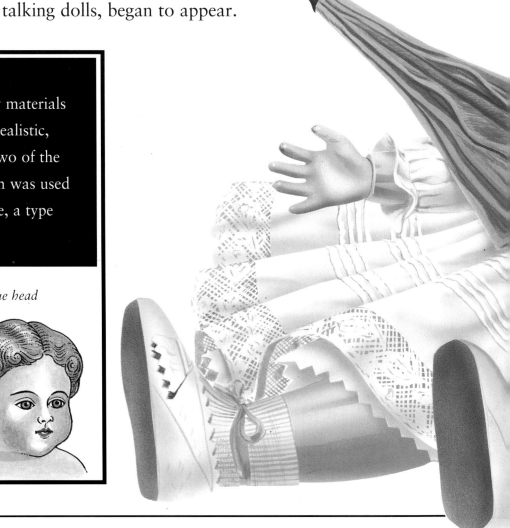

From Ancient Egyptian times to the present day, dolls have been one of the most popular toys of all. In fact, dolls were among the very first toys, although we do not know when the first doll was made. Archaeologists have found ancient figures, made of clay or wood, which may have been ornaments, religious statues or dolls to play with. Greek and Roman dolls had bodies made from wood or clay, sometimes with jointed limbs. Toy manufacturers began to make dolls in large numbers in the eighteenth century. They tried many different materials for making dolls' heads. Wood, wax, papier mâché and various ceramics were all used successfully. Soon, novel dolls with closing eyes, baby dolls that drank from a bottle, and talking dolls, began to appear.

*Lady Arabella Stuart, a cousin of Elizabeth I of England, holding a doll in Elizabethan clothes. Although the little girl is aged only 23 months, it is interesting that her doll is a replica of a lady, and not of a baby or child, like the dolls played with by today's toddlers.*

## TYPES OF HEAD

Doll manufacturers tried many materials to make heads that would be realistic, durable and cheap to make. Two of the best materials were wax, which was used as an outer coating, and bisque, a type of porcelain.

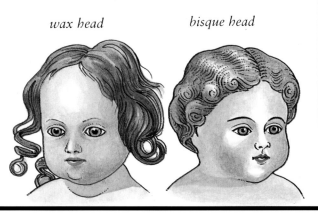

*wax head*          *bisque head*

## TYPES OF BODY

The parts of a doll's body that were hidden under its clothes were normally made in cheaper materials than the head and shoulders, and the lower arms and legs.

*Wooden jointed body with porcelain head and shoulders, forearms and lower legs.*

*Stuffed cloth body with porcelain head, shoulders, forearms and lower legs.*

*Complete porcelain or composition body for a doll sold without clothes.*

*A German doll with a bisque head, made in the late nineteenth century. It has glass eyes and a wig made from mohair.*

## MODERN DOLLS

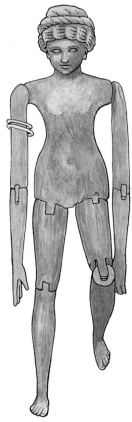

### FASHION DOLLS
*Many different outfits are available for modern dolls, including a wide range of shoes, jewellery and other fashion accessories.*

### RAG DOLLS
*Dolls do not necessarily need to look realistic. Rag dolls can be just as much fun to play with.*

### DOLLS THROUGH THE AGES
The main changes in dolls through the ages have been in the materials used to make them.

Today, you can buy hundreds of different types of doll. Most of them are mass-produced in plastic, which makes a basic doll quite cheap to buy. Wooden and rag dolls are also available, but they have to be made by hand, and so are often more expensive than plastic dolls. Modern dolls can be very simple or very complicated. Some are made from just one or two pieces of coloured plastic, with no moving limbs. Others have fully-moving arms and legs, real clothes and hair that can be styled. Some of the latest dolls even contain electronics and other gadgets that make them talk, cry and wet their nappies. Among the most famous dolls to appear in recent times are Sindy and Barbie. As well as the basic doll, you can buy outfits for every occasion, make-up, cars, houses and even boyfriends!

**200 BC**
*The Romans made some of the first jointed dolls. This one has real gold bracelets.*

**EIGHTEENTH CENTURY**
*Small wooden dolls called Dutch dolls were popular for dolls' houses.*

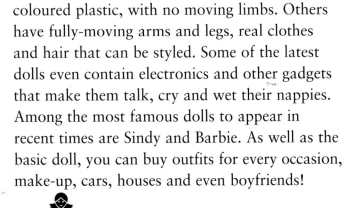

**1878**
The first talking doll was made by the American inventor Thomas Edison. The sound was made by a phonograph, which was the first successful sound-recording machine.

**1990s**
A modern doll made of synthetic materials, such as plastic. She has roller blades, sunglasses and earrings.

## MAKING A DOLL WITH JOINTED LIMBS

**1** Join the outer sleeves from two matchboxes end-to-end with sticky tape.

**2** Cut two arms, two upper legs and two lower legs from stiff card. Using a sharp pencil, pierce holes in the body, legs and arms where the joints will be.

**3** Assemble the legs and attach the limbs by threading strings through the holes and tying the ends.

**4** Paint a face on the doll, and stick on hair made from short pieces of wool or string. Make some clothes as well if you like.

# TOYS THAT MOVE

*JACK-IN-THE-BOX*
*An American jack-in-the-box from the 1950s. It is also a wind-up, tin-made musical box.*

Mechanical toys with moving parts, such as walking dolls, animated pictures and performing acrobats, became very popular in the eighteenth and nineteenth centuries. There were hundreds of different types of mechanical toy. Some were simple, like the balancing toys shown here. Some were more complex, with clockwork power, such as a model man who repeatedly raised a cigar to his mouth. Most expensive were very detailed models of people who performed complicated feats, such as card tricks, completely automatically. These were called automata (see pages 26 - 27), and were really toys meant for adults!

*This swaying figure has counter weights that keep it balanced on its slender stand.*

*Balancing dolls with heavily weighted bases like this weeble-type doll are found all over the world.*

## HOW A BALANCING DOLL WORKS
A balancing doll has a lightweight, hollow body and a round, heavy base. If the doll tips to one side, the weight becomes off-centre and pulls the doll upright again.

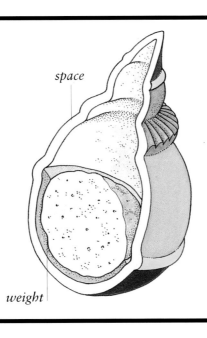

space

weight

*An automaton called the Dancing Punchinello. Winding the handle makes the figure dance, while music plays in the box.*

## MAKE A TIGHT-ROPE WALKER

Counter-weight balancing toys balance because most of the weight of the figure is lower than the point on which the figure rests. You can see how this works for yourself by making this balancing tight-rope walker.

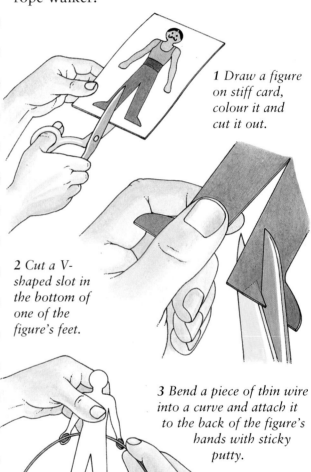

**1** Draw a figure on stiff card, colour it and cut it out.

**2** Cut a V-shaped slot in the bottom of one of the figure's feet.

**3** Bend a piece of thin wire into a curve and attach it to the back of the figure's hands with sticky putty.

**4** Add blobs of sticky putty to the ends of the wire to make the figure balance on a taut string.

## ACROBATS

*A typical acrobat toy. The hands are fixed to the pole which is twiddled by hand to make the figure somersault.*

*The legs are jointed so that they swing freely.*

Simple moving toys had to be operated by twiddling a knob or pulling a string. Some very common examples were acrobats, which swung around a horizontal bar, hammer toys, where two figures hit an anvil alternately, and a monkey on a stick, which worked in a similar way to the swinging acrobat.

## PECKING BIRDS

Another type of mechanical toy was operated by a swinging weight. These toys appeared in the second half of the nineteenth century. You held the toy by its handle and moved it to and fro or round and round to keep the weight swinging. As the weight moved, it pulled on different strings in turn, making different parts of the toy move in turn. Swinging weight toys often showed scenes including people and animals. A well-known example is the pecking birds toy. As the weight swings, the birds peck the ground in turn, making a drumming noise.

### NEW IDEAS FOR MOVING TOYS

Here are a few moving toys that have appeared in the twentieth century. As technology has advanced, and more modern materials have become available, people have been able to make many other simple toys whose appeal for children lies in the way they move.

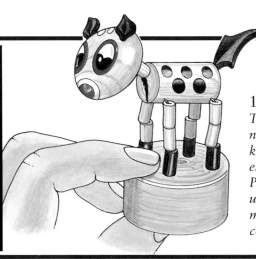

**1950s**
*This toy's limbs, neck and tail are kept rigid with elastic strings inside. Pressing a button under the base makes it collapse comically.*

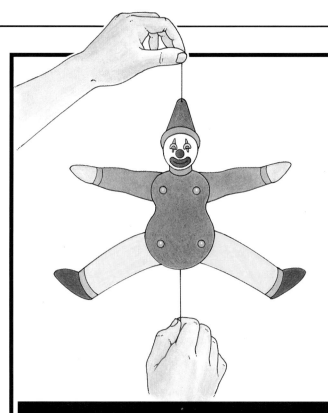

## THE PANTIN

The pantin was one of the most popular toys ever. It was a figure, such as a clown or dancer, with legs and arms which could rotate at the hips and shoulders. Pulling the strings at the top and bottom made the arms and legs rise upwards. The first pantins were made as children's toys, but they soon became all the rage as an entertainment for adults.

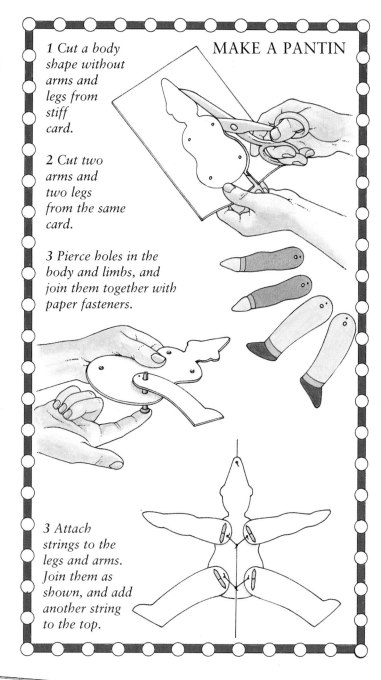

MAKE A PANTIN

*1* Cut a body shape without arms and legs from stiff card.

*2* Cut two arms and two legs from the same card.

*3* Pierce holes in the body and limbs, and join them together with paper fasteners.

*3* Attach strings to the legs and arms. Join them as shown, and add another string to the top.

### 1960s
*The Slinky is a steel or coloured plastic spring that moves down a staircase on its own.*

### 1970s
*Sticky rubber feet keep this window walking toy attached to the glass as it tumbles downwards.*

### 1980s
*Inside this car is a tiny flywheel-powered motor that is wound up by dragging the car across the floor. The car then shoots forwards for a few seconds. This mechanism was invented in the 1940s.*

## HISTORY OF AUTOMATA

Mechanical figures and animals have been made for thousands of years. They were most popular during the eighteenth century. Today, there are very few toys that you simply wind up and watch, except for some aimed at tiny children.

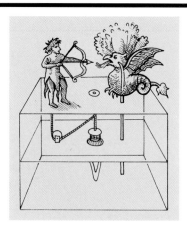

*SECOND CENTURY BC*
*A steam-driven automaton built by the Greek scientist Hero of Alexandria.*

## HOW AUTOMATA WORK

Automata were powered by clockwork. Winding them up normally turned a shaft that caused the model to move. Different methods were developed to make the shaft work other movements, such as the up-and-down movement of an arm.

## SIMPLE AUTOMATA MECHANISMS

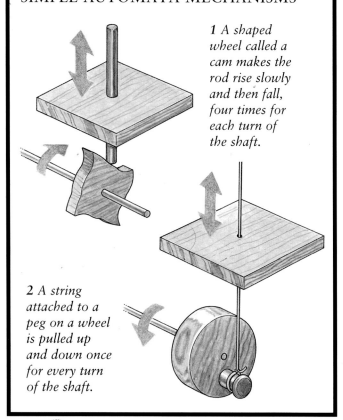

*1 A shaped wheel called a cam makes the rod rise slowly and then fall, four times for each turn of the shaft.*

*2 A string attached to a peg on a wheel is pulled up and down once for every turn of the shaft.*

## AUTOMATA

Automata are moving toys that perform clever feats and actions completely automatically. Simple automata were made in medieval times, but their real rise in popularity came during the eighteenth century. Automata were normally built by watchmakers and clockmakers to show off their skills. The most complicated examples took years to design and make. They were toys for grown-ups to show off to their friends rather than for children to play with, and were seen as fascinating curiosities - museum pieces in their own era.

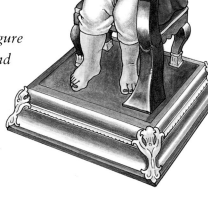

*THE WRITER*
*This mechanical figure writes on paper, and its eyes watch the pen as it moves. The figure was made in the 1770s.*

THIRTEENTH
CENTURY ONWARDS
*Automatic figures were
built to strike the hours
on the front of decorative
church clocks.*

1950s
*Battery-powered walking
robots were made popular
by the interest in science
fiction and space travel.*

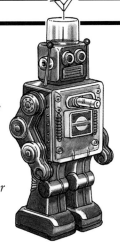

1980s
*This electronic buggy can be programmed
to carry out movements
automatically.*

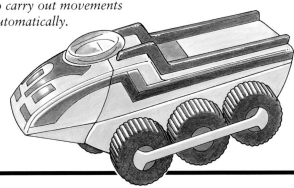

One of the most famous automata makers was
a Frenchman, Jacques de Vaucanson. He made
many automata which were exhibited all over
Europe, where they amazed the people who
flocked to see them. They included a flute player
that played twelve tunes, and a duck that swam
along, drank water, and even ate and digested
food! Not all automata were so advanced.
Simpler ones were mass-produced, mostly made
of tin-plate and with clockwork mechanisms.
Some even used the working principle of an egg-
timer, being powered by falling sand. Many
automata were models of figures that played
musical instruments, lovingly
reproduced in miniature.

## MOVING PICTURES

Moving picture toys were a combination
of a picture in a frame and an automatic toy.

*1 A sand-powered toy.
Falling sand turns a
hidden wheel, making
the monkey's arm move.
Turning the box upside
down for a few seconds,
then the right way up,
sets the toy going again.*

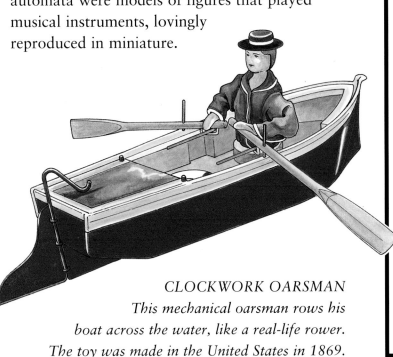

### CLOCKWORK OARSMAN
*This mechanical oarsman rows his
boat across the water, like a real-life rower.
The toy was made in the United States in 1869.*

*2 Other
sources of
power were
clockwork, and even
steam. Here, steam makes
the cat play the violin and the
kittens dance.*

# OPTICAL TOYS

In nineteenth-century Europe, people became fascinated by toys that created some sort of 'magic' optical effect or illusion. These included toys that made photographs or paintings appear three-dimensional, toys that produced recognisable pictures from strange patterns, and toys that produced moving pictures.

One reason that these toys were so popular in the early nineteenth century was that the first successful photographs were now being taken. The interest in toys and other machines that could produce moving pictures led inventors to develop the idea of the cinema.

*A VICTORIAN FILOSCOPE*
*The filoscope was an early kind of flick book. On each page was a frame from a moving picture. Flicking through the book rapidly made the picture seem to move.*

## PANORAMA TOYS

Panorama toys showed pictures of famous events in a new and unusual way. One type consisted of a series of cut-out scenes, set one behind the other, inside a concertina-like tube. When you looked through a hole at one end, the receding frames gave an exciting impression of depth in the picture.

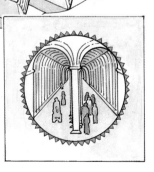

*Long, narrow spaces, such as the insides of cathedrals and tunnels, made good panoramas.*

## THE THAUMATROPE

The thaumatrope was one of the earliest and simplest optical toys. Spinning the disc quickly made the two pictures on the opposite sides appear to combine into one picture.

## THE ZOETROPE

The zoetrope appeared in the 1860s. It consisted of an open revolving drum with narrow slits around the top. A strip of pictures, each slightly different to the one before, was placed inside the drum. You spun the drum and looked into it through the slits. As each slit passed your eye, you caught a glimpse of the picture on the opposite side of the drum. The sequence of pictures created the illusion of movement. Picture sequence discs could also be put in the base for added effect. The phenikistiscope was a flat disc with slits around the edge which worked in a similar way to the zoetrope.

## MAKE A THAUMATROPE

1 On a piece of paper, draw a circle about 10 cm across with the complete picture on it (for example, a jockey on a horse). Mark positions for the two holes for the strings, one at each side.

2 Trace the circle, the hole positions and one part of the picture (for example, the horse). Stick the tracing on a piece of card and cut out the circle.

3 Trace the circle again, with the hole positions and the other part of the picture (for example, the jockey). Cut out the second circle of tracing paper and stick it upside down on the other side of the card circle. Make sure that the hole positions on each side match up.

4 Pierce the two holes and tie a piece of string through each. Twiddle the strings in your fingers to make the thaumatrope work.

# MOVING PICTURE MACHINES

Moving images, such as films and television pictures, are not really moving at all. They are made up of still pictures, called frames, which we see one after the other in quick succession. Our eyes cannot react fast enough to see each individual frame, so we see a moving image instead.

The oldest and simplest moving picture toy is the flick book. This is a small

book with a frame from a moving picture on each page. Looking at the pages while quickly flicking through the book creates the moving picture. Modern moving picture toys and games work electronically. Some of these display pictures on a television or a similar sort of screen, where

*A sequence from a zoetrope. Each frame is slightly different from the one before.*

*Activating sections of an LCD (liquid crystal display) screen one after the other gives the impression that an object is moving.*

## MAKE A PHENIKISTISCOPE

*1 Cut a circle of stiff card about 25 cm across. Using a pencil and ruler, divide the circle into eight equal segments.*

*2 Cut a slot 5 cm long and 1 cm wide at the end of each pencil line.*

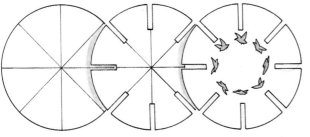

*3 Draw a moving picture with eight frames. Cut out the frames and stick one at the bottom of each slot. The top of each frame must be nearest the slot.*

*4 Push a pencil through the middle of the circle. Stand in front of a mirror and spin the disc. Look through the slots to see the moving picture in the mirror.*

## DEVELOPMENTS IN OPTICAL TOYS

With their brass cases and glass lenses, the first optical toys looked more like scientific instruments than toys. Plastic lenses made them cheaper and more robust.

each frame is shown for a split second. Simple toys, like the one shown here, have a screen like an electronic watch. There are shapes in set positions on the screen. Making these shapes appear and disappear in the correct order creates the illusion that they are moving.

You can find out more about electronic toys on pages 40-43.

You can find out more about electronic toys on pages 40-43.

## HOW A 3D PICTURE TOY WORKS

Three-dimensional picture toys actually display two pictures, one for each of the viewer's eyes. The pictures show a scene viewed from two slightly different places, which is how our eyes actually see a scene. Our brains are fooled into seeing a picture with depth and solid objects, rather than a flat picture.

*Pairs of pictures for 3D viewing are called stereo pictures. Try viewing this example. Put your index finger on the page between the two pictures, and then gradually lift it. Keep looking at your finger, and the two pictures will merge together.*

*1980s TO TODAY*
*Cheap pocket electronic games have small liquid-crystal displays similar to those in electronic watches.*

*1960s*
*This 3D story viewer has interchangeable story discs. Rotating the disc shows the next picture in the story.*

*EARLY NINETEENTH CENTURY*
*The kaleidoscope produces a pattern by reflecting coloured pieces of glass in two mirrors.*

*1860s TO 1930s*
*The magic lantern projects a picture from a slide on to a screen. The light is provided by a paraffin lamp.*

# TRANSPORT AND POWER

Many types of toy are models of real-life things, and some of the most common are toy vehicles. They became popular as new forms of transport, such as trains and cars, were developed during the nineteenth century. Toy manufacturers brought out toy versions of machines very soon after the real things had appeared. The first transport toys had to be pushed or pulled along, but before long, methods of powering the toys, such as clockwork and friction, were invented. Some toys used the same sort of engine as the real thing, but in miniature form. Just as today, some transport toys were cheap and simple, while others were more accurate models, and so more expensive.

*TIN-PLATE TOYS*
*Three tin-plate toy cars. Two were made in Germany in the 1930s, and the other was made in Japan in 1958.*

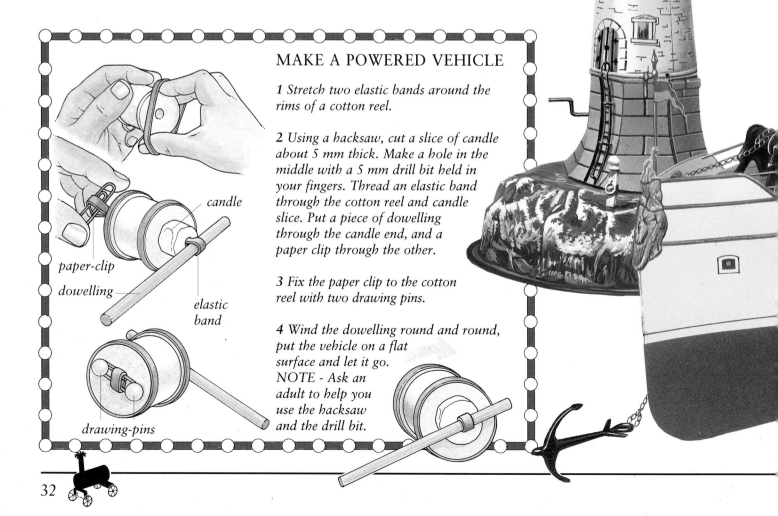

## MAKE A POWERED VEHICLE

*1 Stretch two elastic bands around the rims of a cotton reel.*

*2 Using a hacksaw, cut a slice of candle about 5 mm thick. Make a hole in the middle with a 5 mm drill bit held in your fingers. Thread an elastic band through the cotton reel and candle slice. Put a piece of dowelling through the candle end, and a paper clip through the other.*

*3 Fix the paper clip to the cotton reel with two drawing pins.*

*4 Wind the dowelling round and round, put the vehicle on a flat surface and let it go. NOTE - Ask an adult to help you use the hacksaw and the drill bit.*

candle
paper-clip
dowelling
elastic band
drawing-pins

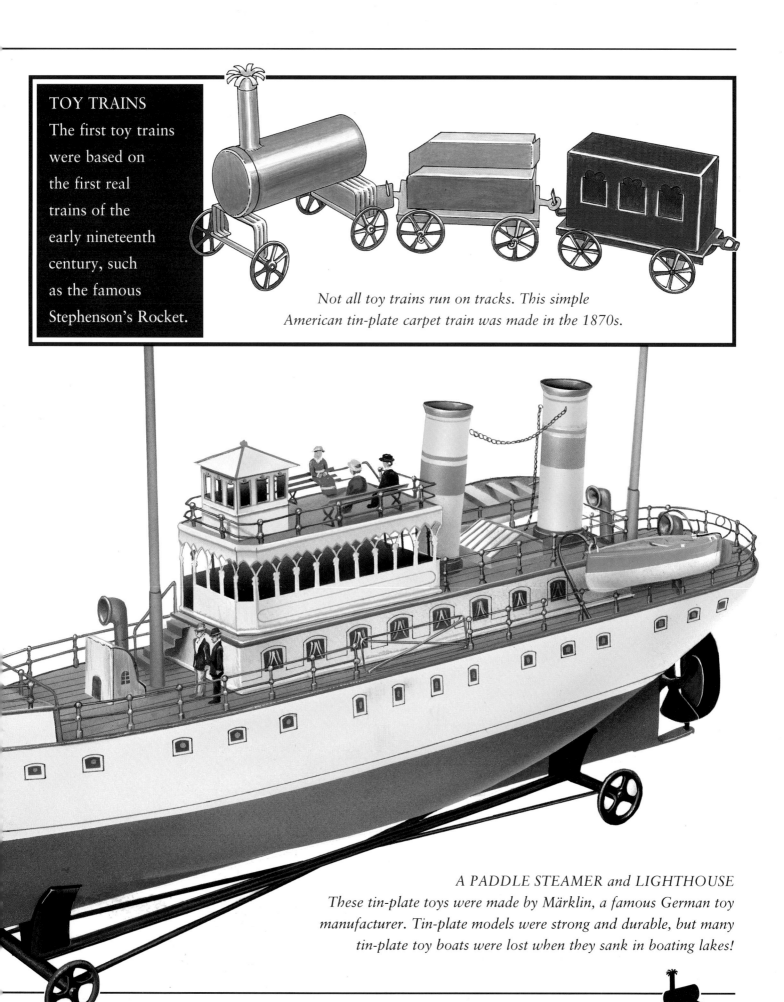

## TOY TRAINS
The first toy trains were based on the first real trains of the early nineteenth century, such as the famous Stephenson's Rocket.

*Not all toy trains run on tracks. This simple American tin-plate carpet train was made in the 1870s.*

### A PADDLE STEAMER and LIGHTHOUSE
*These tin-plate toys were made by Märklin, a famous German toy manufacturer. Tin-plate models were strong and durable, but many tin-plate toy boats were lost when they sank in boating lakes!*

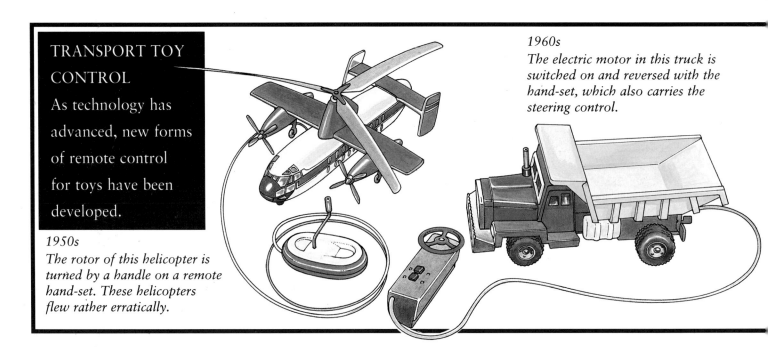

## TRANSPORT TOY CONTROL

As technology has advanced, new forms of remote control for toys have been developed.

*1950s*
*The rotor of this helicopter is turned by a handle on a remote hand-set. These helicopters flew rather erratically.*

*1960s*
*The electric motor in this truck is switched on and reversed with the hand-set, which also carries the steering control.*

## ELECTRIC POWER

Today, electricity is the most common form of power for transport toys. The electric energy is stored in a battery, or comes from the mains, and an electric motor changes the electric energy into movement. The first electric transport toys were toy trains made in the1890s. They ran on batteries that only produced a weak electric current, and their motors were too cumbersome for small models. Small, reliable, electric motors were not developed until the 1930s. By the 1960s, many moving toys had electric motors powered by batteries.

### TRACK POWER
*Modern toy locomotives are controlled by remote control. A transformer can change the amount of electricity in the rails, and so vary the speed of the train.*

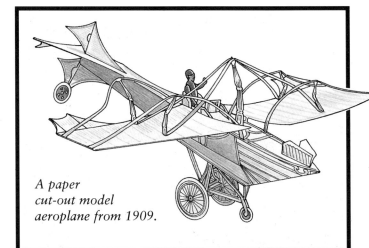

*A paper cut-out model aeroplane from 1909.*

## MODEL AEROPLANES

The first toy aeroplanes appeared at the beginning of the twentieth century, soon after the first real aeroplane flights. The first toy aeroplane that could actually fly was made in 1907.

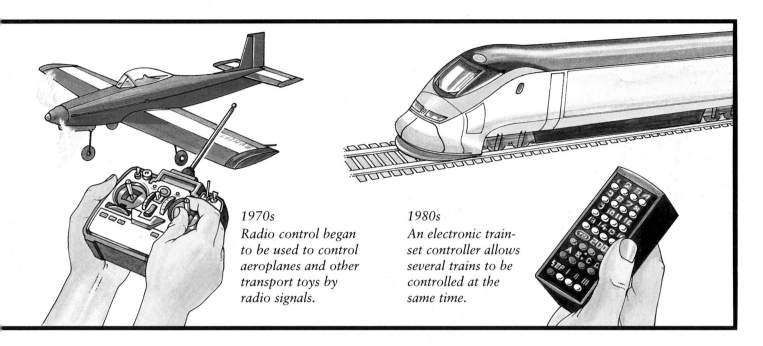

**1970s**
*Radio control began to be used to control aeroplanes and other transport toys by radio signals.*

**1980s**
*An electronic train-set controller allows several trains to be controlled at the same time.*

## MECCANO

Meccano was patented in 1901 by Frank Hornby, who got the idea while studying a construction crane. Meccano parts are still made following the original design so that old and new sets can be used together.

*A motorcycle, complete with shock absorbers, made entirely from Meccano.*

## CLOCKWORK

*A WIND-UP CROCODILE*
*This bath-time toy has a clockwork-powered wagging tail.*

Clockwork is a cheap and simple form of power. Until the 1960s, most transport toys were moved by clockwork and it is still used for some cheap toys. A clockwork toy does not need new batteries every few weeks, and can be played with in water, whereas an electric toy would be ruined. Its disadvantages are that the speed of a clockwork motor cannot be controlled very well, and it needs regular winding.

# PLASTIC TOYS

VACUUM CLEANER TOY
*Modern plastics can be made
in almost any colour, so bright,
colourful toys can be produced
without painting.*

The greatest change ever in toy manufacturing came during the 1950s. This was the time when plastics became widely available. Plastics can be moulded and shaped when they are hot, and become solid when they cool down. One of the precursors of plastic, an artificial material called celluloid, was patented in 1870, and used for toy parts over a long period. But it was flammable, and too brittle for whole toys which might get rough treatment. Scientists began to understand plastics better in the 1920s, and new plastics began to appear. Manufacturing techniques such as vacuum moulding were developed, which allowed plastics to be made into complex shapes. The process of manufacturing plastic items is easily automated, and by the 1950s, plastic toys were being made cheaply and in their millions.

*A LEGO set
showing the range
of shapes that can be made from
plastic. With a little imagination, you can
build almost anything from LEGO sets.*

## USING PLASTIC

There are many different types of plastic, and each one has its own characteristics that make it good for certain jobs.

doll's hair and clothes made from plastic fibres

clear plastic lights

one-piece moulded body

synthetic rubber tyres

## HOW A VACUUM MOULD WORKS

*1 Find a small plastic drinks bottle (330 ml or 500 ml). Unscrew the top. Ask an adult to help you pierce several holes in the base with a bradawl.*

*2 Build up a shape, such as a face, with modelling clay on the bottom of the bottle. Make sure you leave some of the holes uncovered.*

*3 Cut the neck off a balloon and stretch it over the shape.*

*4 Suck the air out of the bottle through the neck. The balloon should mould itself to the shape.*

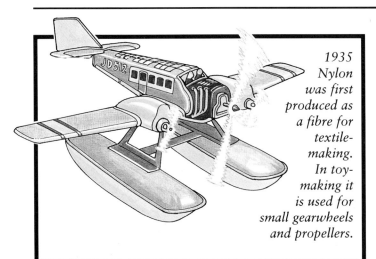

*1935*
*Nylon was first produced as a fibre for textile-making. In toy-making it is used for small gearwheels and propellers.*

Exciting new materials with new properties are being developed all the time. Here are some that are widely used for toys.

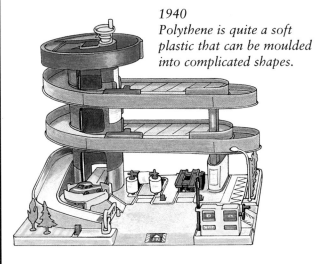

*1940*
*Polythene is quite a soft plastic that can be moulded into complicated shapes.*

*1943*
*PVC can be made into sheets, as used in this play house, or moulded into rigid shapes.*

## CONSTRUCTION KITS

The parts of a plastic construction kit come joined together because they are made in one piece in a mould.

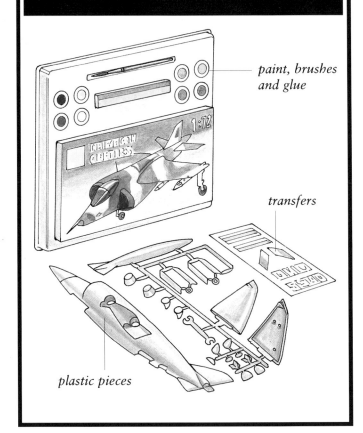

*paint, brushes and glue*

*transfers*

*plastic pieces*

## OUTDOOR TOYS

Plastics are waterproof and hard-wearing, making them ideal for outdoor toys.

*SPACE HOPPER*
*This inflatable toy is made from synthetic rubber, which can stretch and return to shape without being damaged.*

# A CHANGE OF MATERIALS

During the 1950s and 1960s, plastics almost completely replaced other toy-making materials. They replaced tin-plate for making transport toys, because moulded plastic parts could be given much more realistic detail than tin-plate parts, and could be glued or made to snap together. Dolls were made completely from flesh-coloured plastic - these were much more durable and realistic than the china-headed dolls. Wooden seats on outdoor toys like swings were replaced with hard-wearing plastic ones. Small toys, such as dolls' house cups and plates, became much cheaper because they could now be manufactured in plastic in large numbers. Plastic is now the most commonly used toy-making material, but it is not suitable for every job. Metal is used where extra strength is needed, and many beautiful wooden toys are still made for younger children.

## TOY SOLDIERS

*Early toy soldiers (left) were made one at a time from metal or wood. Using plastic, small pieces like soldiers can nowadays be made hundreds at a time. Plastic-based paints make them easy to decorate (above).*

## PEDAL VEHICLES
*Plastic can be combined with other weather-proof materials, like metals, to make ride-on pedal-powered vehicles.*

## GARDEN SLIDES
*Modern plastics like PVC can be moulded into large shapes like the parts of this slide.*

# SPACE-AGE TOYS

Electronic educational toys can help children from four years upwards to learn spelling or arithmetic in a fun way. The machines can 'speak' their questions and answers.

Electronics and computers have had an enormous effect on toy-making, just as they have in many other areas of our lives. The first breakthrough in electronics was the development of the transistor (a type of electronic switch) in 1948. Then, in 1958, the first silicon chip was made. This allowed large numbers of electronic components, such as transistors and resistors, to be fitted into a tiny space. Previously, they had been very bulky and expensive. No one even considered using them in toys. Gradually electronic components and silicon chips became cheaper and easier to produce. By the mid-1970s, they had even become cheap enough to be used in simple electronic toys and games. The first microprocessor was made in 1971. This allowed compact computers to be built and paved the way for the explosion in computer and video games.

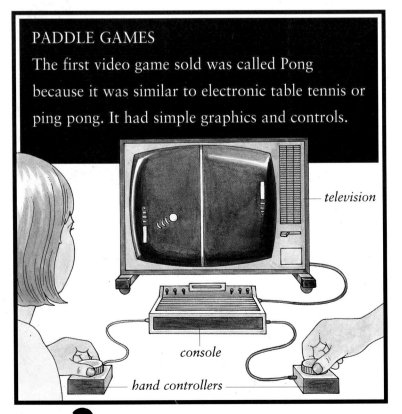

## PADDLE GAMES
The first video game sold was called Pong because it was similar to electronic table tennis or ping pong. It had simple graphics and controls.

television

console

hand controllers

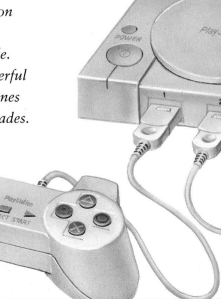

CONSOLES
*The Sony PlayStation is a state-of-the-art home games console. It is almost as powerful as the games machines found in public arcades.*

## SCREENS

*The Sony PlayStation is used with the latest wide-screen television sets, which were pioneered in Japan.*

## DESIGN A HAND-HELD GAME

*You can't make a real computer game, but you can have fun designing one. Make some sketches of your game console. It needs a screen, four direction buttons and some fire buttons.*

## JOYPAD

*Each player uses a hand-held control called a joypad to control the game.*

## TOY SYNTHESIZERS

There have always been toys that are simple versions of things in the grown-up world. Today, children can play with toy synthesizers that actually make music electronically. Some of them have memories and can play back, as well as supplying background melodies. Instruments available include keyboards, guitars, drumkits and saxophones. Many have microphones for singing along, sometimes incorporated in an electronic headset.

*microphone headset*

*guitar synthesizer with built-in recording tape*

# VIDEO GAMES

A video game console is a specialized computer that can draw graphics very quickly on a screen. It is programmed to play different games when different electronic cartridges or compact discs are loaded into it. Instead of a keyboard, the console has a joystick or keypad. You control the game by moving the joystick or pressing the buttons on the keypad. Many video games involve battling with aliens on another planet, fighting the forces of evil in a fantasy land, or finding your way through a series of puzzles or obstacles. During the game, the computer constantly checks your input and works out how this affects what happens to the characters or places in the game. It uses this information to construct the relevant picture on the screen.

*The screen of a hand-held game is actually made up of a grid of thousands of tiny squares. The electronics in the console send a tiny electric current to the squares it needs to darken to make a picture.*

## ADVANCES IN ELECTRONIC TOYS

Since the first simple electronic devices were made in the 1950s, they have quickly become more and more complex. The toys that use electronics have become more complex, too.

*1970s
A simple electronic game. The players must remember the order in which the coloured lights flash, and repeat it by pressing the buttons.*

## VIRTUAL REALITY

Virtual reality is a make-believe world, created by computer, designed to make you think it is real. All the details of the make-believe world are stored in the computer's memory. The world might be a fantasy land, the inside of an ancient building or life on another planet. From the stored details, the computer builds up a picture of what the world looks like from any point of view in it. Wherever you look in the pretend world, the computer draws what you would see. You are fooled into thinking that you really are in the pretend world because the picture is shown in a headset which makes it appear three-dimensional. You press buttons on a joypad to move about in the make-believe world.

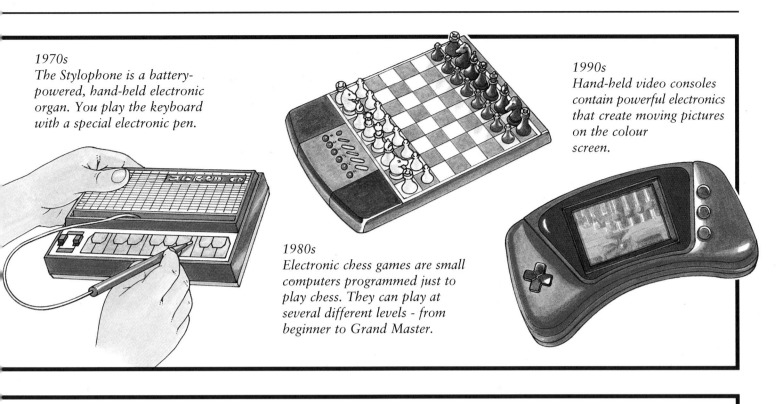

**1970s**
*The Stylophone is a battery-powered, hand-held electronic organ. You play the keyboard with a special electronic pen.*

**1980s**
*Electronic chess games are small computers programmed just to play chess. They can play at several different levels - from beginner to Grand Master.*

**1990s**
*Hand-held video consoles contain powerful electronics that create moving pictures on the colour screen.*

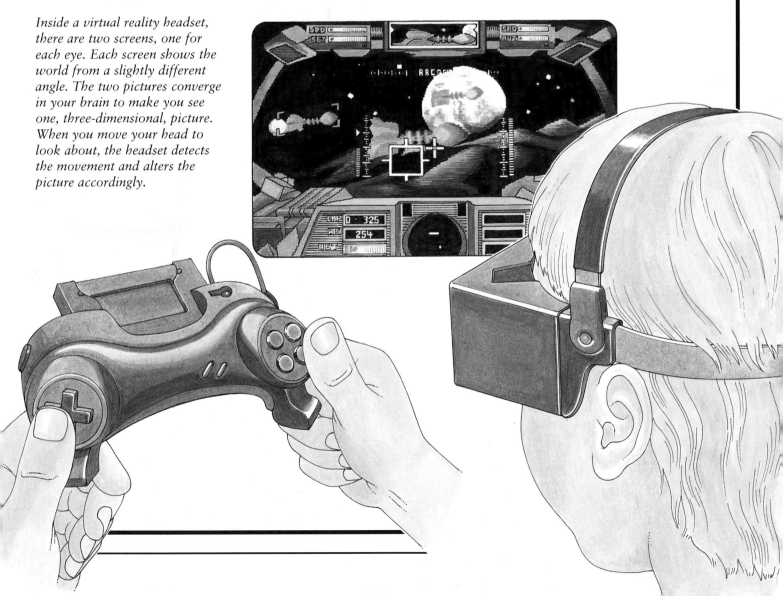

*Inside a virtual reality headset, there are two screens, one for each eye. Each screen shows the world from a slightly different angle. The two pictures converge in your brain to make you see one, three-dimensional, picture. When you move your head to look about, the headset detects the movement and alters the picture accordingly.*

# GLOSSARY

**ARCHAEOLOGIST** A person who studies the past by looking at ancient objects, ruins and scripts.

**AXLE** A rod around which a wheel turns. Axles are used in cars, trains and other vehicles.

**CERAMICS** Another word for pottery, that is, anything made of clay.

**CLOCKWORK** A mechanical device which uses the energy released by a powerful spring to make a clock or toy work.

**COMPONENT** One part of a whole object.

**COMPOSITION** A pre-plastic artificial material developed for moulding dolls' body parts.

**CONSOLE** A control panel used for operating computer games.

**COUNTER WEIGHT** A weight that stops a toy from toppling over by forcing it upright if it begins to fall too far to one side.

**ELECTRONIC** Something which is operated by an electrical circuit, made up of small components such as transistors and capacitors.

**FLAMMABLE** Any material that quickly and easily bursts into flame if you set light to it.

**FLATS** Model soldiers or other figures made from flat pieces of metal, with moulded shapes on one or both sides.

**FLYWHEEL** A heavy wheel that stores energy used to power a toy. You will find flywheels in toys such as model cars.

**GRAPHICS** Drawings or designs produced by hand or by computer. Computer graphics are widely used in computer games.

**GYROSCOPE** A device that resists movement. Inside a gyroscope is a very fast-spinning fly-wheel.

**HOBBY HORSE** A toy horse consisting of a horse's head on the end of a pole. You sit astride the pole to ride the horse.

**MECHANICAL** Something that is operated by a system of cogs or wheels and levers, rather than by electricity or other means.

**MOLTEN METAL** A liquid made when a metal is heated so much that it melts.

**OPTICAL** Anything to do with light and how you see light.

**PAPIER MACHE** Papier mâché (literally, mashed paper) is made by soaking strips of paper in water and paste to make them pulpy and pliable. When it dries, the paper pulp forms a hard material.

**PHONOGRAPH** A device that records and plays back sound. The phonograph was the first recording machine. It is the forerunner of the modern record player.

**PORCELAIN** Very fine, delicate china pottery.

**PROTOTYPE** The prototype of an object is a working version of the object, built to scale. It is used to check whether the final object will work properly.

**SPINDLE** A very thin rod often used to twist or wind thread.

**SYNTHESIZER** An electronic musical gadget that can reproduce the sounds of several traditional instruments.

**SYNTHETIC** Artificial or man-made.

**THREE-DIMENSIONAL** Something that has height, depth and breadth, that is, something that stands out and does not look flat.

**VACUUM MOULDING** A process used to mould plastic sheets into different shapes by sucking them on to a mould while they are soft.

# INDEX